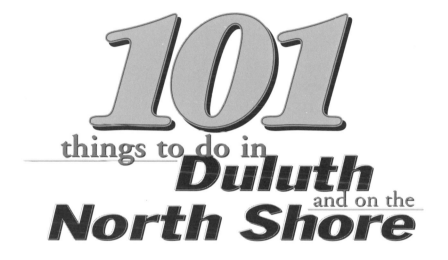

101
things to do in *Duluth* and on the
North Shore

Book and Cover Design by Jonathan Norberg

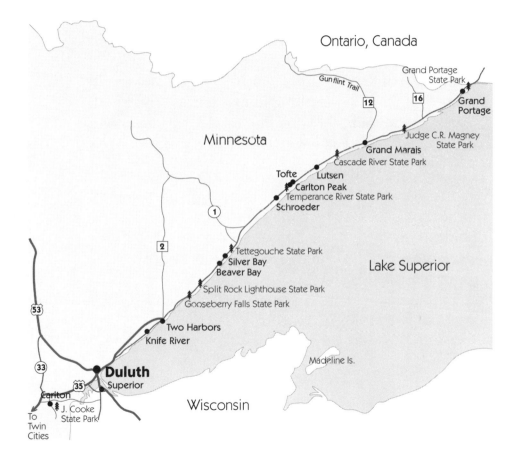

INTRODUCTION

Ease right into your vacation with *101 Things to Do in Duluth and on the North Shore*. These fun suggestions will make your stay in Duluth and on the North Shore enjoyable and stress-free. You'll find everything from the best vantage point for watching thousands of migrating hawks, to where to take your family for a wet and wild day of whitewater rafting.

The suggested activities begin in Duluth and progress sequentially up the North Shore. The index includes important information on all the attractions, so you have everything you need in one easy to use book. Also for your convenience, the Duluth Visitor Centers offer free maps detailing area highlights, and be sure to check out Duluth's informative website at www.visitduluth.com.

Enjoy!

1. First things first. When in Duluth, head straight to Canal Park on the waterfront. Visit the Lake Superior Maritime Visitor Center for the latest news on the giant lake carriers and foreign ships that pass within yards of the center. For year-round information, including ship pictures, log on to the Duluth Shipping News website or call the Boatwatcher's Hotline (see index).

2. Walk across the world-famous Aerial Lift Bridge for a different perspective of the harbor. Notice the bridge's ornate ironwork as well as its interesting counterweight system of operation.

3. Have lunch on the top floor of Grandma's
Restaurant and watch the gulls weave and
dive behind colorful sailboats as they glide by.

4. Hop on the Port Town Trolley (seasonal) for a ride to the historic Fitger's Brewery Complex. Tour their free museum and many shops, then mosey on down to the Brewhouse for a juicy grilled burger and a tall glass of one of the pub's home-brewed ales.

5. What could possibly go better with beer than popcorn? You'll find Dee's Pop A Lot in the Fitger's Mall. Try her strawberry flavor, it's a customer favorite!

6. Stroll the incredible rose gardens at Leif Erikson Park. Have a seat on one of the many interesting benches and enjoy a spectacular view of the Aerial Lift Bridge. (Roses begin blooming in June.)

7. Take a self-guided walking tour of international sculpture and art along the waterfront. Brochures available from the Visitors Bureau or the City of Duluth Public Arts Commission.

8. Buy an oversized, blueberry-packed muffin and a large mug of French roast at Amazing Grace Bakery & Cafe located in the DeWitt-Seitz Marketplace. Relax on their terrace under trees strung with twinkling lights and listen to the nearby splash of the fountains.

9. Step on the pressure pedal of the old-fashioned drinking fountain found on the sidewalk along Canal Park Drive. Nothing beats good cold water on a hot day.

10. Score some points with your kids by taking them to Grand Slam for some Laser Tag or Krazy Bumper Kar fun. Try your luck in a batting cage or on the 18-hole King Arthur miniature golf course.

11. Head indoors for a brisk walk through Duluth's skywalk system and wave to the crew at KDLH Channel 3. You'll find them in a glass-enclosed office near the Radisson.

12. Swim high above Lake Superior at Twin Ponds beach located on Skyline Parkway near the Enger Park Golf Course. There's playground equipment on site for the young and those who are young at heart.

13. Play a round of golf on what feels like the top of the world at the Enger Park Golf Course. As you concentrate on a birdie, don't forget to look up now and then for the real thing. Nearby Hawk Ridge is a popular migration route for thousands of birds.

14. Take a drive on beautiful Seven Bridges Road. Wind through the forested hillsides and over seven stone bridges. Explore caverns and spectacular waterfalls.

15. Get your binoculars out for some serious and plentiful bird watching at Hawk Ridge Nature Reserve. (Rated one of the nation's top ten viewing spots for hawks.) During a recent fall migration, observers sighted more than 85,000 hawks. Naturalists are on hand to answer your questions from late August to mid-October.

16. Take a leisurely 90-minute ride on the Lake Superior & Mississippi Railroad as the vintage cars trace a scenic route along the St. Louis River.

17. Dine at the Radisson's Top of the Harbor revolving restaurant. Get the full harbor/city view from 16 floors up.

18. Clip-clop along the waterfront cuddled together in a romantic horse drawn carriage (seasonal). You'll find River's Bend Carriage across from Grandma's Restaurant in Canal Park.

19. Book an evening cruise with Synergy Sails. Be right there on the water as the sun sets, transforming Lake Superior into a magnificent sea of liquid fire.

20. Wine Cellars Inc. offers a thousand different vintages from all over the world for your choosing. If you're having trouble making a selection, they host complimentary wine tasting every Friday evening from 4-7. Find them in the Fitger's Brewery Complex.

21. Love pizza? Love trains? Well, put them together for a 2½-hour ride aboard the North Shore Scenic Railroad Pizza Train. Departs from downtown at The Depot.

22. Cheer on the hometown baseball team at historic Wade Stadium. The Dukes play over 40 regular season home games, facing opponents such as the St. Paul Saints.

23. Hold onto your sides so they don't split from laughter while enjoying the hilarious shenanigans of the troupe from Renegade Comedy Theatre. Weekend shows include improv teams competing for your laughs, as well as comic productions.

24. You haven't truly experienced Duluth until you've cruised under the Aerial Lift Bridge aboard one of the boats from the Vista Fleet. See lake freighters and ore docks up close on this narrated tour.

25. Learn how paper is made on a guided tour of Stora Enso, Duluth Paper Mill. Pick up your free tickets for this hour-long tour at the information center on Harbor Drive by the Vista Fleet. Note: You must be at least 10 yrs. old to take this tour. Tours given summer months on Mon., Wed., Fri.

26. Bring your ideas to The Pottery Studio on Canal Park Drive and they'll turn them into a unique souvenir that lasts forever.

27. Hunt down a treasure at the Canal Park Antique Mall, or head over to the award-winning Blue Heron Trading Company found in the DeWitt-Seitz Marketplace. Featured in *Better Homes & Gardens* magazine, the Blue Heron specializes in kitchen gadgets and flavored coffees.

28. Try your luck with the slots at Fond-du-Luth Casino and if they don't treat you right, take a shot at stardom at the Red Lion Bar on karaoke night.

29. Take a drive along Duluth's historic east end and marvel at the miles of grand old mansions, or better still, book a room in one of them. Many operate as bed and breakfast hotels.

30. Put on some comfortable shoes and grab a map for a walking tour of Duluth's architecturally and historically rich neighborhoods. Free maps found at the information centers.

31. Tour the harbor from a bird's-eye view with Scenic Seaplane Rides. The airport is at the end of Park Point.

32. Want a good idea of what small feels like? Paddle a kayak alongside a docked lake freighter on a trip offered by the University of Minnesota Duluth through their Outdoors Program. Other trips such as cliff climbing are also offered; call for current listings.

33. Examine original historic documents, including the Proposal Draft Bill of Rights and Wagner's own draft of the Bridal Chorus ("Here comes the bride"), at the Karpeles Manuscript Library Museum. Free admission.

34. Climb aboard the S.S. William A. Irvin, a retired 610-foot iron ore carrier. An hour-long guided tour leads you through the ship from bow to stern and includes the engine room, pilot house, crew's quarters and the impressive state rooms with their working gas fireplaces.

35. Let the kids captain an ore freighter through the canal or create massive waves of destruction at the Great Lakes Aquarium, America's only all-freshwater aquarium.

36. See snow leopards, Siberian tigers, Australian kangaroos, Arctic polar bears and many other animals from around the world at the Lake Superior Zoological Gardens.

37. Order a picnic-to-go from The Greenery/Bridgeman's in the Holiday Center, then head for Bayfront Festival Park. The kids will have a blast on all the cool playground equipment while you put your feet up and relax.

38. Rainy day? No problem. Take in a show at the OMNIMAX Theatre. The megalarge screen and advanced sound system make you feel as if you're part of the action.

39. The railway docks extend over 2000 feet into the harbor. Get a good view of the ship loading operation from the observation platform at 35th Ave. W. and Superior Street.

40. Want to take something home besides a fish story? Then charter a day-long fishing excursion on Lake Superior. Catch lake trout, Atlantic salmon, steelheads, walleyes and more. Charter trip brochures available at visitor centers, as well as a long listing of names and detailed information on the Duluth website.

41. What do all kids love? Toys! Take your gang to the Duluth Children's Museum located in The Depot for some hands-on learning and fun.

42. The Lake Superior Brewing Company offers a tour of their brewery at noon on Saturdays and best of all, you get to sample their hearty, handcrafted ales!

43. Tour the Tweed Museum of Art located at the University of Minnesota Duluth. The museum houses one of the finest collections of Hudson River Valley School and American Impressionist paintings, as well as the Glenn C. Nelson International Ceramics Collection.

44. The Duluth Union Depot is itself a historic artifact and a fine Chateauesque-style example of architecture. Inside you'll find heritage and history rooms, an art gallery, and the transportation and children's museums.

45. The Glensheen is a luxurious, 39-room Jacobean-style mansion with formal gardens, a carriage house, clay tennis court and a gardener's cottage. It's also the 1977 site of the brutal double murders of heiress Elisabeth Congdon and her nurse. Summer tours of the mansion conducted daily.

46. Treat yourself to a gourmet dinner and a wonderful performance at Bennett's On The Lake in the Fitger's Brewery Complex. Want to feel like you're part of the action? Then make reservations for one of their audience participation murder mysteries!

47. Are the kids getting a little travel antsy? Then stop the fussing by tuning your radio dial on AM 970 Radio Disney; the station just for kids.

48. Bike from Carlton to Duluth on the scenic Willard Munger State Trail. Over 14 miles of paved trail cuts through rocks, woods and over bridges and gorges. A high bridge overlooks an awesome gorge. Ends near the zoo. Note: Biking back is uphill, so you may want to have a car waiting.

49. Get wet and wild rafting the St. Louis
River on a Superior Whitewater Raft Tour
in nearby Carlton.

50. Drop a line off the Minnesota Slip Drawbridge (the unique blue bridge next to the S.S. William A. Irvin) and fish for lake trout.

51. Pay quiet reverence to the Vietnam
Veterans as you stroll past their memorial
on the Lakewalk.

52. Give a friendly wave to the mounted police who roam the Lakewalk on horseback during the summer months.

53. Stretch out on seven miles of sandy beach along Park Point (accessed by the Aerial Lift Bridge) or walk to the remains of the 1857 Superior Entry Lighthouse.

54. Scenic Highway 61 hugs the Lake Superior shoreline and offers breathtaking views. Notice the abundance of wildflowers and butterflies in the ditches along your route.

55. Want to know how lumberjacks used to do their work without the aid of power tools? Then stop in at Tom's Logging Camp, an authentic, full-scale replica of an early logging camp.

56. Knife River Village is the smoked and fresh fish capital of the North Shore. Have an old-fashioned good time at a Friday night fish boil in the rustic setting of Emily's Store, Inn & Deli.

57. The DNR Fish Hatchery is a great place to learn about cold water fish like trout and salmon. Take a free, self-guided tour of their visitor center and rearing building April through October, but don't expect to see any large fish. The hatchery only handles the babies!

58. The town of Two Harbors offers the best view of giant ore carriers as they load. Head for the waterfront where you can also tour the 1886 tugboat Edna G., the last coal-fed, steam-powered tug to work the Great Lakes.

59. You can't get a real feel for the history of Two Harbors without visiting the Depot Museum. Explore the vintage locomotives next to the museum.

60. Take a guided tour of Minnesota's only operating light station at Lighthouse Point in Two Harbors. If you decide you'd like to stay a bit longer, go ahead. The lighthouse is also a bed and breakfast!

61. Two Harbors is the birthplace of Minnesota Mining and Manufacturing. Their first office, built in 1898, is now the only sandpaper museum in the world. Don't miss a tour of the one-of-a-kind 3M/Dwan Museum complete with hands-on interactive programs.

62. Named one of the world's top 25 trails, the Superior Hiking Trail presents 200 miles of rugged and challenging territory. However, the waterfalls, hidden river valleys, wildlife and majestic views are worth the extra effort. (There are many access points for the trail along Hwy. 61; watch for signs.)

63. Want to hike a trail without doubling back for your vehicle? Then hire the weekend services of Superior Shuttle. They'll give your doggie a ride too!

64. Oh my, it's time to make a stop at Betty's Pies! Dig into a huge wedge of Bumbleberry à la mode or a slice of Five Layer Chocolate. But then again, Cherry Crunch is hard to beat. With more than 50 kinds of freshly baked pies to choose from, the decision is indeed difficult.

65. Gooseberry Falls is Minnesota's most visited state park. It boasts five waterfalls and an outstanding visitor center which includes a gift shop and naturalist programs.

66. There is nothing quite as unforgettably spectacular as the brilliant reds and golds of the leaves during a Minnesota autumn. Breathe in the colors and let the magic live in your soul, but don't forget your camera! (For peak fall colors, call the MN hotline: 800-657-3700 ext. 131.)

67. No North Shore trip is complete without a visit to the Split Rock Lighthouse. Constructed long before Highway 61 gave access to this impressive site, learn how the lighthouse came to sit atop the 130-foot, 2 billion-year-old cliff.

68. Beaver Bay is the oldest settlement on the North Shore and a great place to buy some world renowned Minnesota wild rice. What a delicious souvenir to take home.

69. The beaches along the North Shore are very popular with agate collectors. Get some expert advice about the best hunting spots from the folks at Beaver Bay Agate Shop. They literally have a ton of rocks on display, as well as many impressive specimens of petrified wood.

70. Buy a double scoop of your favorite ice cream flavor from the fire engine red London Transport bus in Beaver Bay. Have a leisurely visit with the other folks who are also standing around licking their cones.

71. Buy a treasure or sell some junk at the Second Hand Rose, an outdoor flea market located on the northern fringe of Beaver Bay.

72. Sip a cup of espresso on the outdoor deck of the Captain's Cove. Enjoy the lake view as you decide on one of the Grampa Woo excursions: scenic and dinner cruises, luncheons and scuba diving. Celebrate your decision with a slice of cheese cake.

73. Take a short stroll on a boulder path out to an island at East Beaver Bay. Bring along some popcorn to feed the gulls.

74. Dying to find out how a taconite plant operates? Then take a free 90-minute tour of the Northshore Mining facility in Silver Bay. Tours offered every Tuesday, Thursday and Saturday at 10 and 2.

75. If a picture is worth a thousand words, one shot taken from the top of Palisade Head could fill an entire book. The 350-foot high palisades offer sweeping views you won't forget. On a clear day, see if you can spot the Apostle Islands a mere 30 miles away.

76. The Baptism River flows rapidly through Tettegouche State Park creating three waterfalls. Rugged hiking trails take you on a self-guided tour of six inland lakes, an early 1800s camp and the 60-foot High Falls.

77. Want to get away from it all? Book a stay in one of the four rustic log cabins on Mic Mac Lake in Tettegouche State Park. The only way to get there is by foot or mountain bike. Is that far enough away for you?

78. Hike the easy half-mile trail along the Caribou River up to the falls. The root beer colored water is due to the region's vegetation.

79. There's no shortage of perfect skipping stones at Sugarloaf Cove. Just grab a trail guide from the mailbox in the parking area and start walking. Let the haunting call of the Minnesota loon lead your way.

80. Visit the granite Father Baragas Cross at the base of the Cross River or view a roaring waterfall from the highway bridge at Schroeder.

81. Cascades, cauldrons, giant potholes and thick forests. If you like these things, then take a hike through Temperance River State Park.

82. Get high on a view in every sense of the word. At 927 feet above lake level, a hike to Carlton Peak located just west of Tofte puts you at the highest point on the North Shore.

83. For centuries, fishing provided a livelihood and way of life for the hardy North Shore folks. Listen to their stories and see original skiffs at the North Shore Commercial Fishing Museum in Tofte.

84. Twist and turn down a half-mile of hairpin curves seated on a plastic sled. This scream of a ride known as the Alpine Slide is a summer attraction at Lutsen Mountains.

85. For breathtaking views of Lake Superior and the bordering mountain ridges, take a two-mile gondola ride at Lutsen Mountains. Especially beautiful during the fall leaf season.

86. Ride the trails through the Poplar River Valley on a horse rented from Homestead Stables located at the Caribou Highlands Lodge (Village Inn & Resort) in Lutsen. Hop on a trolley wagon pulled by a team of Belgian draft horses for an evening campfire sing along.

87. Within a one-mile distance, the Cascade River drops 225 feet in a series of waterfalls and frothing rapids. Hike 15 miles of scenic trails in the Cascade River State Park, then come back in the winter to cross-country ski more than double those miles!

88. After a day of hiking, you'll be hungry enough for Clifford's Goober Burger at My Sister's Place in Grand Marais. Peanut butter and mayo on a grilled beef patty. Yum! The restaurant also offers 21 other burgers for the choosing.

89. The Gunflint Trail officially begins in Grand Marais and leads to some of the greatest canoe country in the world. Pack a lunch, rent a canoe or bring your own, then off you go on an exploratory journey through unspoiled wilderness.

90. Go berry picking to your heart's content along the public trails and wooded back roads. Gather blueberries, strawberries and raspberries in luscious abundance. (Avoid picking along bike trails or main roads as they may be sprayed with herbicides.)

91. Buy a piece of incredible artwork at Sivertson Gallery Art of The North. Find them in the yellow log cabin across from Boulder Park in Grand Marais.

92. Walk out to the end of the pier and watch the waves slap against the breakers at the Grand Marais lighthouse.

93. Order an old-fashioned chocolate soda at Leng's Soda Fountain & Grill, but throw your watch away because these folks tell you straight out, "We are good food, not fast food."

94. Next door to Leng's is the famous Sven and Ole's of gourmet pizza fame. Be brave and try the lutefisk pizza.

95. Cool off with a couple of laps in the huge Grand Marais indoor swimming pool complete with diving board. Open daily, there's also a wading pool, whirlpool and sauna. Campground with summer interpretive programs, recreation center, marina and pavilion nearby.

96. Pamper yourself with a stay on the shores of Lake Superior at Naniboujou Lodge. The bright Cree Indian colors and native rock fireplace give the Great Hall a festive feel. After a scrumptious evening meal, stroll down to the lake for a cozy bonfire beneath the stars.

97. Wake to the aroma of Naniboujou's melt-in-your-mouth blueberry pancakes, homemade rolls and freshly brewed coffee. Order a lunch box to go and spend the day exploring the mysterious Devil's Kettle found in nearby Judge C. R. Magney State Park. This is one of the strangest waterfalls you'll ever see!

98. Established in 1731, Grand Portage became Minnesota's first white settlement. Watch birch bark canoe making and learn all about the town's history from costumed interpreters at the Grand Portage National Monument.

99. Book a boat ride to Isle Royale National Park through Grand Portage Isle Royale Transportation Line, Inc. Spend the day on the island fishing, hiking and exploring, or pack a tent and stay the weekend.

100. You can look across the Pigeon River into Canada at Grand Portage State Park. The park also boasts the impressive 120-foot High Falls and is definitely worth a roll of film.

101. Spend a reflective moment gazing over the coves and pristine islands that dot Lake Superior at any of the many scenic waysides. Hear the Earth's strong pulse in the crash of the waves and experience her glowing life force surrounding the trees. You're suddenly more alive than you've ever been and your soul dances in celebration.

INDEX